UNFURLING

Ian Adams is a poet, writer, photographer, artist, Anglican priest and retreat leader. He is the author of *Cave Refectory Road* and *Running over Rocks* and creator of the daily Morning Bell on social media. Ian is a director of StillPoint, a project seeking to nurture contemplative spiritual practice, and a partner in the Beloved Life project exploring how spiritual practice may change the world. He lives in South Devon.

UNFURLING

Ian Adams

Juno
You can trust the path

Ian

CANTERBURY
PRESS
Norwich

First published in 2014 by the Canterbury Press Norwich
Editorial office
3rd Floor, Invicta House,
108–114 Golden Lane

Canterbury Press is an imprint of Hymns Ancient and
Modern Ltd
(a registered charity)
13A Hellesdon Park Road, Norwich,
Norfolk, NR6 5DR, UK

www.canterburypress.co.uk

British Library Cataloguing in Publication data

A catalogue record for this book is available
from the British Library

978 1 84825 645 3

Typeset by Regent Typesetting, London
Printed and bound in Great Britain by
Ashford Colour Press, Gosport, Hants

For Gail

CONTENTS

PREFACE   ix

RUN BAREFOOT   1

AND IN WE DOVE   2

ANGEL TREE   3

UNFURLINGS I   4

UNFURLINGS II   5

UNFURLINGS III   6

UNFURLINGS IV   7

UNFURLINGS V   8

UNFURLINGS VI   9

UNFURLINGS VII   10

RESILIENT BETWEEN THE STONES   11

EASTBOUND 27 JANUARY
(HOLOCAUST MEMORIAL DAY)   12

HAIKU BEATITUDES: 10 SONGS FOR
A NEW WORLD   13

WAN DOWN DARK-CIRCLED   15

ABSOLUTION   16

SONG OF SONGS 1/8   17

THE GREAT MOUNTAIN   19

EMBERS OF LONG BURNED OUT STARS   20

SO LET IT BE TO ME   21

FIERCE PLAINCHANT   22

RUST IS BEAUTIFUL   24

ABBA JOSEPH IN THE DESERT   25

NINE VOICES   26

NO WRONG PATH 28

PRAYER FLAG 29

DEVOTIONS: PRIME (ON WAKING) 30

DEVOTIONS: TERCE (MID-MORNING) 31

DEVOTIONS: SEXT (MIDDLE OF THE DAY) 32

DEVOTIONS: NONE (MID-AFTERNOON) 33

DEVOTIONS: VESPERS (EARLY EVENING) 34

DEVOTIONS: COMPLINE (BEFORE SLEEP) 35

DEVOTIONS: NOCTURNS (IN THE NIGHT) 36

A STORM IS COMING 37

TO BECOME A PRAYER 38

THE UNBOUNDED OCEAN 39

THE TEACHER'S SEED KOANS 40

MADONNA OF THE FOILS 41

ONE BEAUTIFUL IDEA 42

TACK INTO THE TIDE 43

SOME SLOW EPIPHANIES 1/ 44

TONIGHT I WILL GO TO THE SEA 46

WE ARE ONE 47

SEEKING THE CHRIST OF ST IVES 48

FROM THE ASHES 50

BLISS 51

ISLAND SONGS 1/ 52

THERE'S A RIP 53

JUST ONE MORE WAVE 54

THE LOVE CHILD OF SOME UNKNOWN
GRACE 55

THROUGH CLOUD WORDS 56

NOTES 57

PREFACE

To make a poem is to attempt a holy thing, asking what it means to be truly alive. From a season or a moment of attention a single image or idea seems to emerge, a gift should the poet find the courage to work with it. A seed in the hand. Then the task begins – by turn perplexing, demanding, joyous and even blissful – to find words shapes and patterns that may enable that image to gift itself far beyond its origin. Both poet and reader-hearer may, of course, be changed by the poem. The seed dies, new shoots emerge, new seeds are scattered. As we discover the poem, the poem discovers us.

If there is a thread that runs through these poems it is an instinct that if our world is to rediscover her harmony and peace, such a rediscovery needs to begin within us. Through loving attention to the sacred presence in all that exists – to the earth and its creatures, to the people around us, to ourselves – we may begin to rediscover our deep at-oneness. This may gradually come to be experienced as an unfurling from all the fears and anxieties that keep us bound.

And so may all unfurl.

RUN BAREFOOT

Tender, could we learn
once more to run
as lovers
landing soft
with tender feet?

To take off our shoes
and run barefoot to
trust our toes
and sift the sand
sense the stones and
take the shred, the bruise and cut
to feel the red soil pulse again
and run as our ancestors ran
so light on earth's dust skin;
the beginning of some sweet recovery
and the shedding
of more than shoes,
the softening
of more than tread.

AND IN WE DOVE

Under darkening sky
we sat on the jetty
Aurora sparking skin to skin
the lake our unknown life lapping before us
and the flickering of our stars
as if we were the only ones.

And in we dove
a first dive into love
whose depth we could not know;
the smooth and fearless dive of the young
into water warmed by summer days' sun;
we surfaced as one
gasping for breath
brushing cool skin.

And in we dove.

ANGEL TREE

Meet me down by the Angel Tree
we'll walk the dune path to the sea
with all the lovers who have ever
cried the other's name in whispers,
exchanged beach stones, and shoreline flowers
this is for you – sea's generous favours
and pray with all who have fallen tender
into each other *may this be forever*.

UNFURLINGS I

1
Find your stillpoint, dawn
of your belovedness; now
rise into new day.

2
Shape something simple
strong and beautiful; swallow's
nest from mud and grass.

3
Does the rising sun
seek applause? Devote yourself
to your intention.

4
Start with whatever
is before you: light and stone,
chisel in your hand.

5
The practice is not
the thing; the thing is what the
practice reveals: Light!

6
Bring your unfurling
to the world each day: a sun-
flower opening.

UNFURLINGS II

7

The human story
is shaped each day by you: sow
seeds, carry flowers.

8

Brutality all
around; softening begins
here, pebbles rolled smooth.

9

The well of goodness
can never run dry; fill your
bucket, drink and pour.

10

Will you build a barn,
fill it with straw: or fly in
and out, swallow free?

11

Into what shape will
your mouth settle in old age?
You decide today.

12

The poetry is
all out there, the poem just
a hint – look around!

UNFURLINGS III

13

Dive the gap between
content and discontent: deep
creative river.

14

The future is not
somewhere else but here and now:
sunlight, rain dancing.

15

Stop trying to prove
yourself; become a swallow
in flight; blur of joy.

16

Change in Syria
or the next Syria starts
here: with me, with you.

17

Into the rising
wind the kestrel bites her wings;
holds her head so still.

18

When it comes, as it
will, let the breeze of summer
warm you, all you need.

UNFURLINGS IV

19

You are loved, live as
beloved; dragonflies in
embrace, dance in light.

20

When hate storms, leaves you
reeling: seek the love within
that will keep you free.

21

Resist the urge to
throw rocks or hurl boulders: *skim
stones*. Your peace brings change.

22

You ask how to love
this world? See how light persists,
winter afternoon.

23

It's easy when it's
easy; stay true when it's hard,
head into the storm.

24

Trust the unfurling;
in your bold hands let the work
discover itself.

UNFURLINGS V

25

Beware acclaim's warm
comfort; seek only to be
filled with light, *all flame*.

26

Never enough for
your striving: always enough
gift, autumn leaf fall.

27

Study the conflicts
within you; know them, be free;
flock flying as one.

28

Those failings? Just your
clumsy attempts to come home:
the door stands open.

29

Miles brings the trumpet
to his lips: *So What!* Some day
all will be dancing.

30

Flowers graffiti
the pavement. Could our work be
to notice beauty?

UNFURLINGS VI

31

Recall the moment
today, as sun on your face.
Let it warm you now.

32

The track unmarked on
the map may be the road you
need: follow it home.

33

As you sleep, wisdom
will stir, reveal what you seek –
waiting within you.

34

What if your great task
is simply to become a
good human being?

35

You do not lie down
alone. An echo from each
star: *with you always*.

36

You can trust the path
from dust to ashes; hint of
greater becoming.

UNFURLINGS VII

37

Deep in the belly
unseen, new life stirs, seeding
flowers into spring.

38

Why stare back at routes
you did not take? Walk the path
that waits, through mountains.

39

A mistake may lead
by path unimagined, to
a clearing, light streams.

40

Whichever path you
choose (or none – which is one) tread
soft, red deer, woodland.

41

Old man gasps his last
breath; new-born gulps her first breath:
spirit passes on.

42

As an eagle, soar
over the earth: ride the winds
of her compassion.

RESILIENT BETWEEN THE STONES

Looking down
and breaking up
on a day of broken things:
folds of shy green moss
resilient between the stones
sitting soft with such
generous welcome,
catching all my shards,
their edges shining.
So I look up.

EASTBOUND 27 JANUARY (HOLOCAUST MEMORIAL DAY)

Eastbound in a crowded
carriage. Facing back (a
seat I had not chosen)
watching the railway track
sliding west; the sunlight
too recedes through grey trees
thinned arms devoid of leaves.
A mist is falling down
the hill onto flooding
fields. A high fence and lamps
on posts surrounding sheds
with rooflights or chimneys?
Then smoking towers. And
a cold sky without birds.

HAIKU BEATITUDES:
10 SONGS
FOR A NEW WORLD

1

Blessed are the poor
in spirit: in them shines the
dawn of a new world.

2

Blessed are those who
mourn: in them will rise the warmth
of spring, consoling.

3

Blessed are the meek:
they amazed shall inherit
the earth, common land.

4

Blessed are those who
hunger and thirst for right: through
them justice, clear rain.

5

Blessed are those full
of mercy: from them flows love's
healing, wide river.

6

Blessed are the pure
in heart: shone-through clarity.
They will see the Love.

7

Blessed are the peace-
makers; golden threads of light
under brooding skies.

8

Blessed are the ones
persecuted for goodness:
night sky, pulsing stars.

9

You are the salt of
the earth: so become wild sea
spray, sharp cleansing storm.

10

You are the light of
the world concealed: so step out
from the tree-line, *shine*.

WAN DOWN DARK-CIRCLED

Some winter-cold days the sky lifts surprised,
teased by a hint of spring to come, screwed-tight
hills begin to unfold, faded soil reds
again, and the estuary floods with light.

But this greyed winter's sky has fallen low,
hard into the hollows. Light elusive,
a fragile animal curled small and slow
on her soft self, some cautious fugitive

rarely emerging from her den, daring
to be glimpsed at the cloud line's low edges
fleet in the lights of a speeding van, in
breaking reflections from tide-filled ditches.

So, wan down dark-circled I leave the house
to seek her. And should I find this creature
I will cup her gentle in my hands lest
she, half-awake, is spooked by my darkness.

ABSOLUTION

Hear the salt sharp words
of absolution shaken
over you:
this is a new day...

SONG OF SONGS 1/8

1

Let this Song of Songs
– which is yours – into your heart:
gift to all lovers.

2

Kiss me on the lips
and keep on kissing me on
the lips: soil and sun.

3

I just say your name –
and the scent of you fills the
room, clear drops spring rain.

4

I see how others
desire you: do you have room
hidden for our love?

5

Dare I ask: can you
see beauty beyond my hurts,
as I gaze on you?

6

Under rings, piercings
and tattoos, your skin shimmers:
I keep on gazing.

7

Lie down here with me;
blossom falls on a summer
morning, as we dreamed.

8

Evening blur, swallows
swoop all around us: in your
eyes such playful flight.

9

This bed and this room:
our love's far horizons; we
will not be leaving.

10

Some day I will let
this truth touch me: Beloved
is mine, I am his.

THE GREAT MOUNTAIN

Still night clouds on the sea-loch. A quiet
lapping under the hull. I trail my hand
in the cool water. Slowly, hint of light,
a pencil-thin line to the east; the sun
dreaming warmth into our cold arrival.
The sail starts, snaps and shimmers a greeting
and the boat tugs, stretching from the long night.
We stir, and pull down the hoods from our heads.
The Great Mountain begins to fill with light.

EMBERS OF LONG BURNED OUT STARS

as if the swirling cosmos
is pivoting
on this one moment
in this one place
breath-held
we stand entranced by
embers sparking from the fire
fluttering all around...
they sway and spin and settle
upon us
illuminating our faces
in their fragile light paths
drawing us into some deep recognition
you, me, us!
and timeless from across the worlds
as lovers' hands have always done
our hands brush and touch and hold
and now we
the embers of long burned out stars
spark and flutter
sway and spin and settle
upon each other

SO LET IT BE TO ME

The child will be holy
she whispers
So let it be to me.

This mother
whose suffering
will only be eclipsed
by the joy of the bright morning star,
the boy she is nurturing in her womb
and to whom she will soon give birth
a birth like every other,
unlike any other.

Lifted up will be the lowly
she whispers
So let it be to me.

FIERCE PLAINCHANT

1

My arm around you
last thing before sleep: so night
comes, calm under clouds.

2

The way you await
the sun-warmed moment, then swim
out beyond your depth.

3

This unguarded place
of trust, each pause, each movement:
eyes lock: you are loved.

4

You catch me looking
at you, imagine something
wrong; but all *so right*.

5

Tell me your story.
Tell it all. Winter beach hut,
squalls, light, solitude.

6

Tell me your story
once more. Paths you took, rivers
crossed, fields you slept in.

7

Running loose to what
binds, you dip skinny in cold
sea: your breath caught, freed!

8

You are loved: a slow
undulating song between
us, our fierce plainchant.

9

Your hair up I see
the scar on your neck; healing's
tender tattoo, life.

10

An old-fashioned set
of scales; lightest of weights placed –
and so we balance.

11

Your turning toward
the sun, your folding into
night: such happiness.

12

Your absence surges
through me. The stones are silent,
the trees say nothing.

RUST IS BEAUTIFUL

A discarded drain cover
wears warm and tender
on a south-facing beach amongst rocks
long removed from its place of work
now discovering its Paschal task:
to reveal in its transformation
that rust is beautiful.

ABBA JOSEPH IN THE DESERT

Stumbling through a scorched stream-bed
a black-clad figure, spirit-led
descends once more into arid accidie
where dreams fall away from unsteady feet
thoughts spike the soul's soft skin
and promises circle those who break them.

The Abba stops. Stands, arms outstretched.
In the wind-silence of the desert,
ever higher in the sky the sun's
searing focus is now on this one man
consumed by the fire – a lens
through whom you too may burst into flame.

NINE VOICES

1

Always want to be
right? Welcome the sudden down
pour, catching you out.

2

If you need to be
needed, walk in the wood; she
needs no one, but loves.

3

When you must win at
all costs, defeat may come as
generous nightfall.

4

You desire to shine,
lone star? See the Milky Way
burst – myriad stars!

5

If you have to know
pray for friend cloud-unknowing
to envelop you.

6

Longing for safety?
Walk the vast plateau: risk all
under a big sky.

7
Do you always flee
pain? Look the fearsome creature
in the eye: fear's fear.

8
Called to fight monsters?
Take care not to grow monsters'
claws; stand as mountain.

9
When it seems too much
follow one breath with your love,
and then another...

NO WRONG PATH

There is no wrong path
except the path
taken
with regret
without love
in anger or from fear.

It's how we take
the path we choose.
How we breathe
into each step, loose
and free, and look up
with expectancy;
how we greet each fellow
traveller we meet;
and leave no record
of our passing there
bar the aroma of
just-extinguished prayer.

PRAYER FLAG

Unfurl a prayer flag for what is now
and for whatever may become
let it flutter then snap and slap in the breeze
offering its fragile plea to the wind
until one day it shreds
to the single strand
of your hope,
for one frayed thread
may be enough to move mountains.

DEVOTIONS: PRIME
(ON WAKING)

1

You: my beginning
and my ending; sun's arc from
dawn till dusk each day.

2

So could it always
be like this? Sunlight-wakened,
your name on my lips.

3

We run together:
fewer words, shared rhythm, the
sound of our breathing.

4

Wet grass around our
feet: *Do not hold on to me.*
Why so reticent?

5

I unfurl the mat
in cool morning air; so now
may I be unfurled.

6

I will seek the best
– *Kyrie Eleison* –
in others, in me.

DEVOTIONS: TERCE (MID-MORNING)

7

Healing light streaming
between all things – Daystar you
reveal our shining.

8

Today, every
day: our death, our burial,
our resurrection.

9

A coin in the mouth
of a fish: *tell me who do
you say that I am?*

10

Morning sun on wild
meadow in flood – cathedral
doors flung wide open.

11

You watch entranced as
Hepworth sculpts the warm stone: *yes!*
All becomes divine.

12

Sensing the dance, earth
and heaven, many and one,
we take off our shoes.

DEVOTIONS: SEXT
(MIDDLE OF THE DAY)

13

At last, warmth on my
face: so behind the clouds you
were shining, always.

14

Becoming present:
bread and wine, earth and labour,
taste still on my lips.

15

As Messi spins and
swerves you catch your breath – a pass
that cuts you open.

16

Amongst all the noise,
you are here, the quiet voice
not speaking; the pause.

17

Always you seek us
with tenderness; curious
robin in winter.

18

Not hidden so much
as so bright – summer noon sun –
I cover my eyes.

DEVOTIONS: NONE
(MID-AFTERNOON)

19

Walking the tidal
road; ebbing tide, autumn sun –
Love calls love: *meet me.*

20

You enthralled as Bach
scores B Minor mass: beyond
your imaginings.

21

So still, so fluent;
estuary winter light,
skein of geese fly south.

22

Your hand sweeps the dust,
opening space for me to
write a new story.

23

A pause, heavy with
hope for a glimpse of birds in
paradise. Wing beats?

24

Learning as lovers
do, to slow our pace, and walk
together in time.

DEVOTIONS: VESPERS
(EARLY EVENING)

25

Your invitation:
Come and see. In a sea mist
the path disappears.

26

As Picasso paints
Guernica you mourn: children –
what have we become?

27

Our stories meet yours,
streams into a great river,
then the unseen sea.

28

Place of grace, saints dance
around the table; unseen
companions – *with bread.*

29

Cool evening coast walk
seeking you; incoming tide,
you are seeking me.

30

Wondering why your
voice so quiet – but could we
bear such blissful jazz?

DEVOTIONS: COMPLINE (BEFORE SLEEP)

31
Today, another
step on the pilgrim path: how
soft has been my tread?

32
Most days just ebb, flow
with my tide-table prayers.
Then, a high spring tide.

33
A room fragrant with
frankincense, wounded open
hands, *Peace be with you.*

34
Kneeling, I slowly
look up and find you gazing,
at me, curious.

35
Amazed: could you find
your oneness in me as I
find oneness in you?

36
You: my ending and
my beginning; sun's sleep each
night from dusk till dawn.

DEVOTIONS: NOCTURNS
(IN THE NIGHT)

37

In the storm, can just
make out your words carried on
the wind: *follow me.*

38

Game of hide and seek;
your outline in the curtain –
I rush, you have gone.

39

So many voices;
but I hear most clearly in
the gaps between them.

40

Flailing in darkness
I grasp for your name. Slowly
a rhythm, calming.

41

I return to the
machair: wind, salt and flower-
censed with your wild dreams.

42

In each slow deep breath,
your life: so ever deeper
I will draw on love.

A STORM IS COMING

The hint of a line darkening
the western horizon. A bleed
of ink seeping toward us. Cool
gusts of wind shake the sharp dune grass.
It hisses. A wave breaks high up
the beach, and almost catches out
a small flock of sanderling, but
they sense its surprise and take flight.
You shiver and pull tight the cords
of your hood; we look at each other.
A storm is coming.

TO BECOME A PRAYER

After all the words are said
let yourself become
the mat unfurled
the candle lit
the ikon kissed
the breath drawn
the quiet air prayed in.

THE UNBOUNDED OCEAN

Always looking for calm water –
but calm may only be found in a pond.

The unbounded ocean
is where I must
become at home
with its
breaks and troughs
with its
rips and sheens
with its
storms and swells.

THE TEACHER'S SEED KOANS

1

To produce the fruit
yours to gift: fall dead as seed
in winter's ploughed field.

2

On the breeze, seeds for
a new world: can you become
their fertile green field?

3

Wheat and weeds in the
same field: how may the wheat be
enabled to thrive?

4

The smallest of seeds
becomes a great tree; shelter
to all that need home.

5

In belly unseen,
darkest soil nurtures what is
waiting to emerge.

MADONNA OF THE FOILS

In a halo of foils
waiting for colours to take
the madonna stares
into the mirror
in deep reflection
recovering her quiet strength
from some unspoken sadness:
scissor cuts into the soul.

ONE BEAUTIFUL IDEA

For weeks I had sat by the pool till late
each night, the practice of a poet's faith
return each day to the source of it all
but nothing moved as darkness fell.

Tonight I watched again as the sun set
behind the trees, and in the shadows' rise
and light's slow cease, the dance of hatching flies,
in this clear moment I saw – or sensed

one beautiful idea, sharp from the sea
beyond belief if I'd not seen her leap
sleek from the deep peat pool, silver goddess
and of wise earth's gifts it's said, the oldest.

I'd begun to think her gone forever, a story
we had caught and caged, and then ignored
but she was here sign of earth's resilient life
and grace for the practice of this poet's faith.

TACK INTO THE TIDE

To cross the estuary
tack into the tide.

The stronger the stream
the more bold must be
the angle of your approach,
hard into what is pushing you
off course.

Then the moment of re-orientation:
a subtle touch on the tiller
letting the flow carry you
to the shore
guiding you
home.

1

I write to learn how
to fly, lifted on rising
breeze, over mountains.

2

I am loved; how strong
this sense, how fragile: a leaf
falling in autumn.

3

There's not very much
I wouldn't do for you if
you say you love me.

4

What is it I see
in your eyes that could make me
return to the wild?

5

To a man of peace
a shock: found myself sliding
into pit of hate.

6

Moments when the world's
beauty is overwhelming:
I catch breath, see stars.

7

Some nights foreboding
rushes in, deepening storm
front. I fight for breath.

8

Would have so loved Eight
but Seven is blissful: *thank
you* Sibelius.

9

Always returning
from some Atlantic; will I
find my river home?

10

I can't be fearless
but I can choose to be bold.
Break this pupae-skin.

11

The deeper I go
into the forest, the more
joy seems to be choice.

12

The beautiful world
is already here: look up
into falling rain.

TONIGHT I WILL GO TO THE SEA

Tonight I will go to the sea.
And sit on the beach
where we used to sit.
And I will take off my scarf,
my jacket and shirt
my boots and jeans.
I will remove everything.
Except your ring,
and my Tau cross.
Tonight I will walk into the sea.

WE ARE ONE

Maybe we are not so different after all;
for in the uneasy truce
of held-back words and pragmatic silence
that has fallen winter-cold between us
we are beginning to see that
our scars and bruises
though from different sources
may connect us in deeper patterns
disclosing that
you are my sister and my brother
and that we are One.

SEEKING THE CHRIST OF ST IVES

So could you be one
of us? Today I seek the
Christ of St Ives. Are

you the man seeking
your recovery; morning
coffee a prayer?

you the young mother
on Porthmeor in seaside hoops,
all is blue and cream?

you the young child sat
spellbound by the sand running
soft through your fingers?

you the pastel-mac'd
woman laughing with friends – of
childhood holidays?

you the builder, top
off, guns out, banter with mates –
last night's escapades?

you the bold swimmer
who could not ignore the call
of the blue-green sea?

you the worshipper
sitting back against the wall
eyes closed, warming sun?

you the wet-suited
surfer, running the sand as
if the swell might drop?

you the one writing
this poem in the café;
so many questions?

You are all of these –
and much more. The Light between
us, Light within us!

FROM THE ASHES

You have spent a lifetime
quietly mourning or ignoring
your losses and your lostness
with no funeral, no wake and no way
to nurture your joy.

Time for a burial.
No, for *a burning!*
For a great funeral pyre
that will light the night sky.
Then a festal meal of bread and wine.
And, from the ashes, perhaps some kind of rising.

BLISS

The way that you give everything
for the pearl of great price –
diving into the sea of your deep past
breathing hard into the breath that sustains you
surfacing into the sunlight of your becoming.
Bliss.

ISLAND SONGS 1/

1
See the islands: Skye
Muck Canna Rum and Eigg – all
is light, all are one.

2
Over the great slow
earth, a sea eagle circles;
we dance in her trail.

3
An ancient stone cist
on the headland; sit with me,
bury your losses.

4
Almost stumble, stop!
A nest, daring on the ground,
three mottled gulls' eggs.

5
Under rock pool glass,
seaweed shimmers: rolled up sleeve,
I choose a colour.

6
Wisdom of Black Monks
in warm stone: seek cat stillness,
monkey fluency.

THERE'S A RIP

There's a rip in the fabric of my favourite shirt
and gradually it is fraying
a thread unravelling
that will one day
unpick the shirt
and return it back beyond
its cotton source:
into earth, water, light
and only the memory of its wearing.

JUST ONE MORE WAVE

Will this wave be remembered? Or
is it just one more wave breaking
on rocks, rising lost in falling
only the haul of the fallen
the discarded, holed and splintering
to mark the surge and its passing.
The moon still pulls, the earth revolves,
the tides ebb and flow. And waves
will always break here, returning to Source.
Will this wave be remembered?

THE LOVE CHILD OF SOME UNKNOWN GRACE

I was the love child of
some unknown
Grace Kelly.

I had seen a picture in a magazine so
I knew I had her eyes, her hair, was sure
I was her everything and one
summer day she would return
with the story of our forced parting
and our beautiful reconciliation
and she would hold my face
to hers and whisper
never again.

Years later, the winter truth.
Would you like to know your name?
A girl and a boy in a park
last of the fallen leaves
cold rain off the Irish Sea.

Then, some slow unfurling epiphany:
still I am the love child
of some unknown Grace.

THROUGH CLOUD WORDS

Forget all I have said.
Remember only
splashes of light refracted
through cloud words,
falling tender.

NOTES

Page 24 The word 'Paschal' refers to the suffering, death and resurrection of Jesus the Christ. In the Church calendar the Paschal mystery is celebrated each year at Easter, and in the weekly Sunday Eucharist.

Page 25 Abba Joseph of Panephysis was one of the so-called Desert Fathers, the first monastics in the Jesus tradition.

Pages 30–36 Prime, Terce, Sext, None, Vespers, Compline and Nocturns are a version of the traditional monastic hours of prayer during the day and night.